KENNER BOOGIE

Written by
JON BATISTE

VOCAL/PIANO

Jon Batiste
Hollywood Africans

Due to licensing restrictions, "Green Hill Zone"
is not included in this folio.

ISBN: 978-1-5400-5024-3

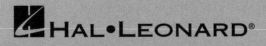

Visit Hal Leonard Online at
www.halleonard.com

Contact us:
Hal Leonard
7777 West Bluemound Road
Milwaukee, WI 53213
Email: info@halleonard.com

In Europe, contact:
Hal Leonard Europe Limited
42 Wigmore Street
Marylebone, London, W1U 2RN
Email: info@halleonardeurope.com

In Australia, contact:
Hal Leonard Australia Pty. Ltd.
4 Lentara Court
Cheltenham, Victoria, 3192 Australia
Email: info@halleonard.com.au

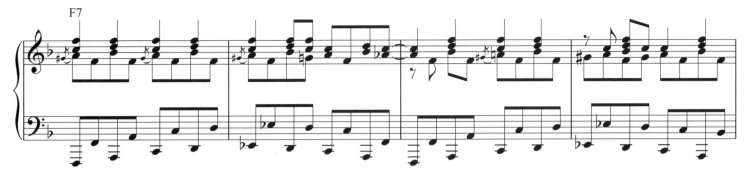

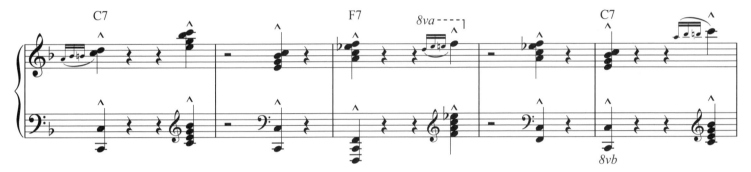

6

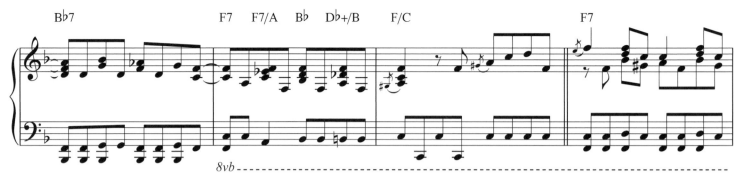

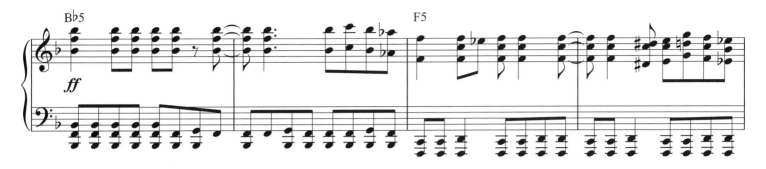

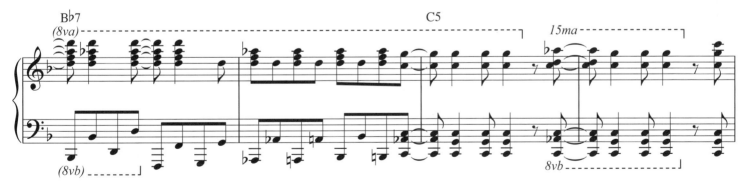

WHAT A WONDERFUL WORLD

Words and Music by
GEORGE DAVID WEISS
and BOB THIELE

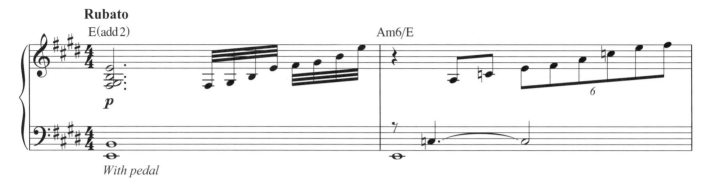

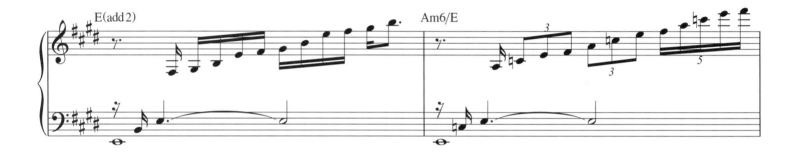

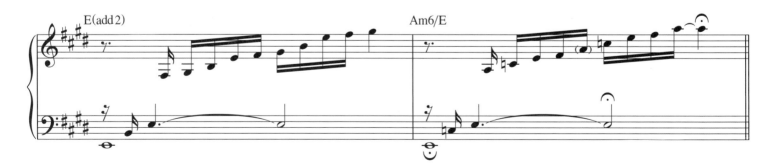

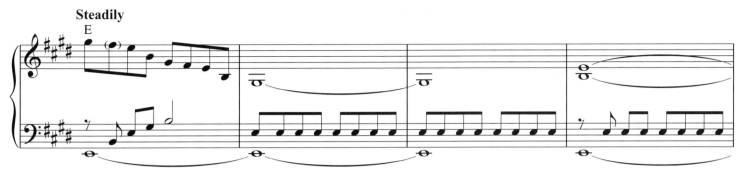

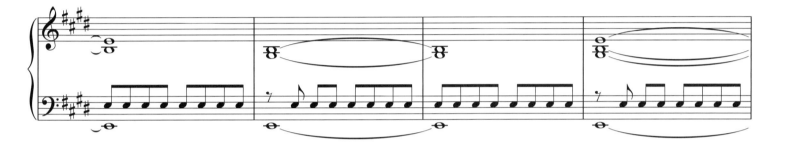

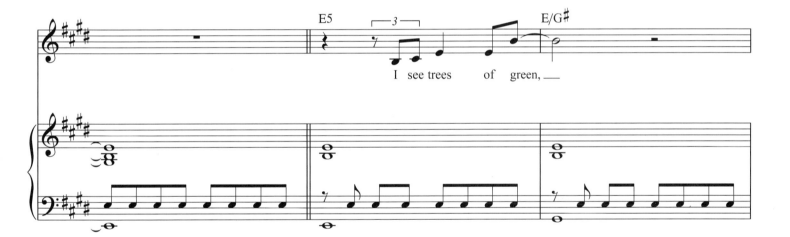

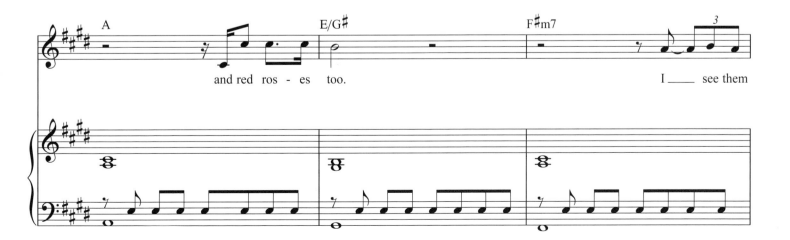

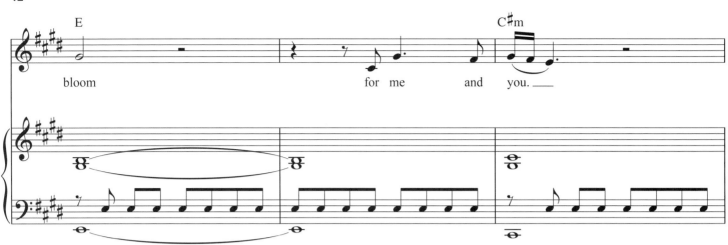

bloom   for me   and   you. ___

And I think   to my - self, _____

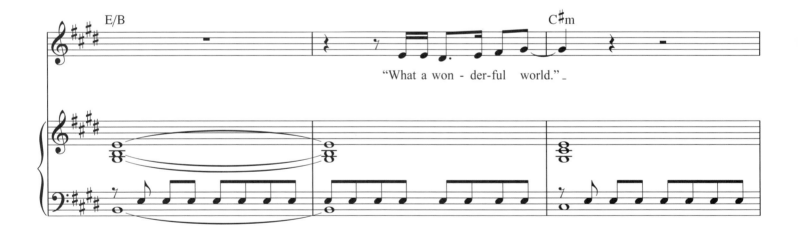

"What a won - der-ful   world." _

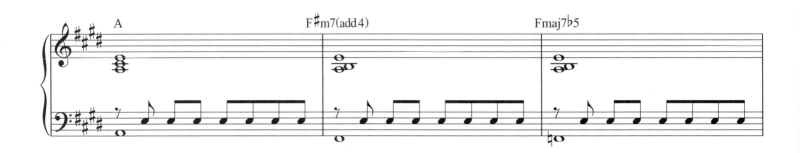

"What a won - der - ful world." _

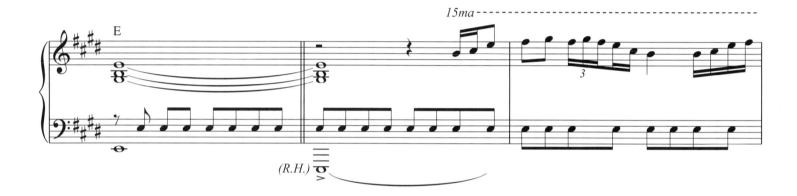

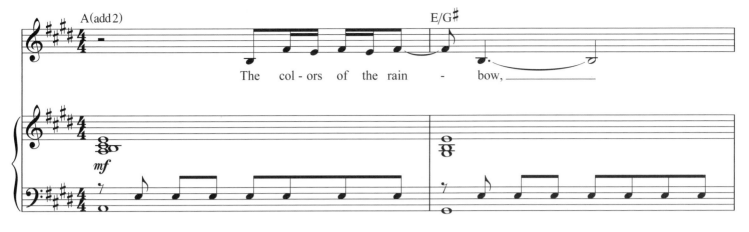

The col-ors of the rain - bow, _____

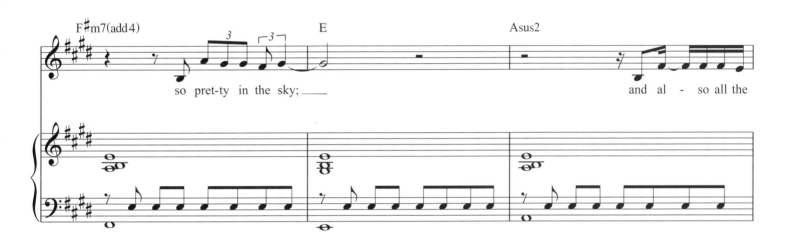

so pret-ty in the sky; _____ and al - so all the

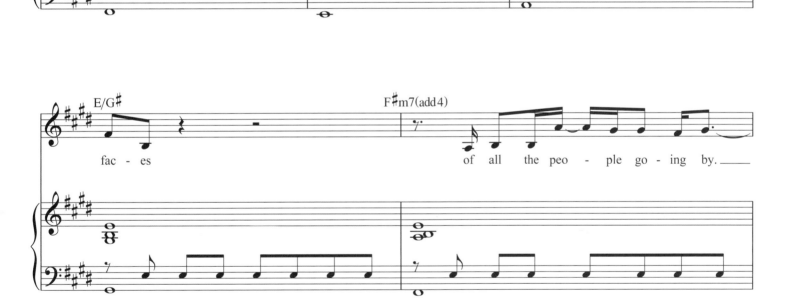

fac - es of all the peo - ple go - ing by. _____

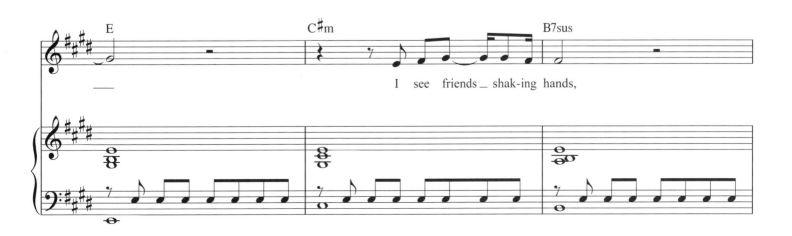

_____ I see friends ___ shak-ing hands,

say - ing, "How do you do?"

They're _ real - ly say - ing, "I love you." _

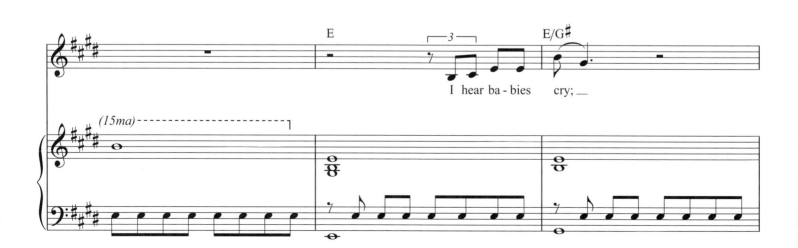

I hear ba - bies cry; _

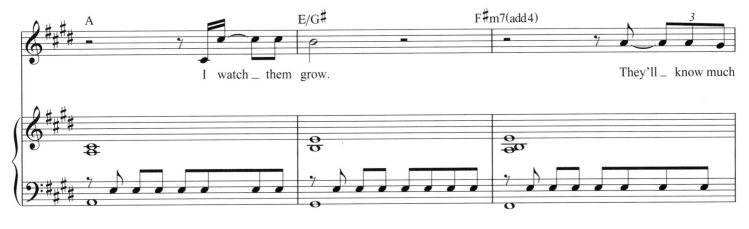

I watch __ them grow.   They'll __ know much

more _____   than I'll _____ ev - er   know. _____

And I think to my - self,   "Self,

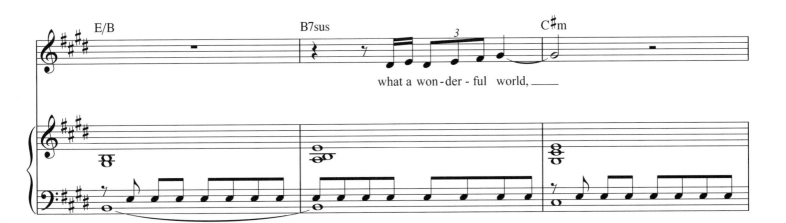

what a won - der - ful world, _____

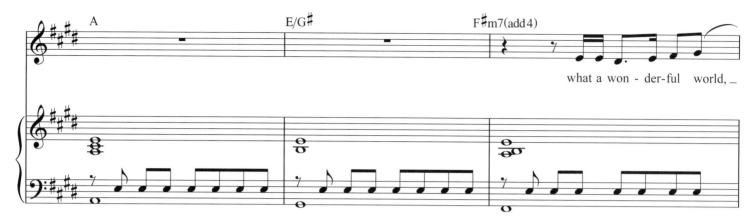

what a won - der-ful world, __

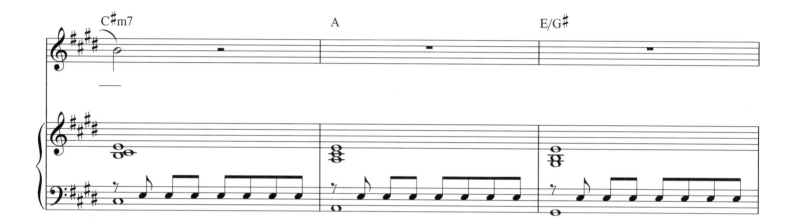

what a won - der-ful __ world, _____

what a won - der-ful __ world. _____

CHOPINESQUE

Written by
FREDERIC CHOPIN
and JON BATISTE

Slowly and freely (Rubato)

Very slowly

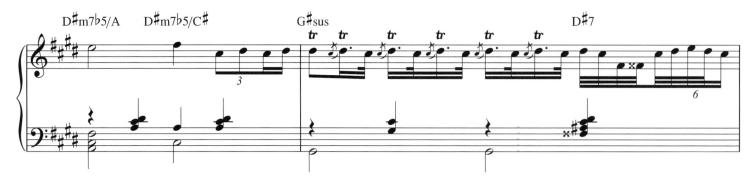

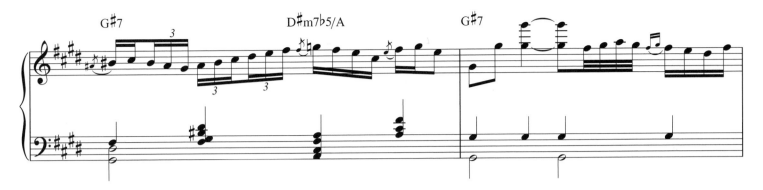

With more motion

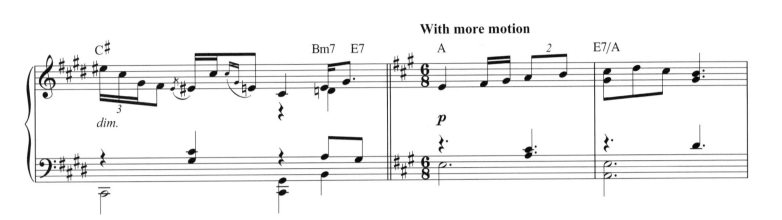

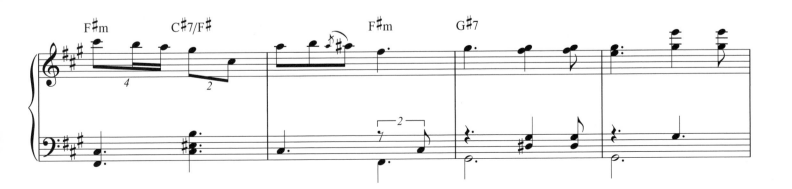

Slowly

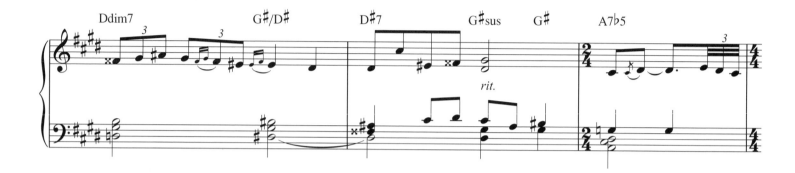

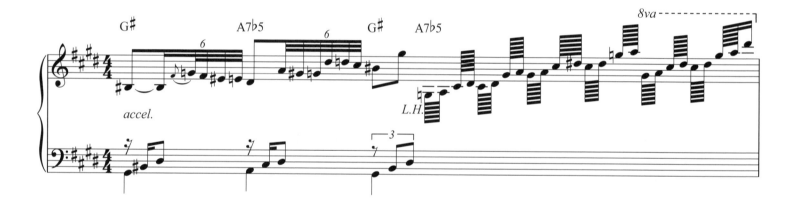

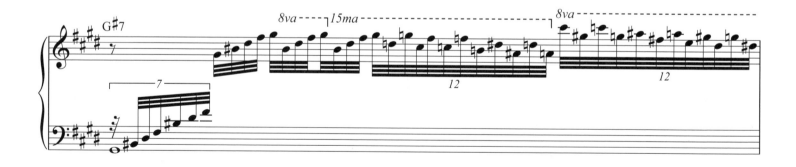

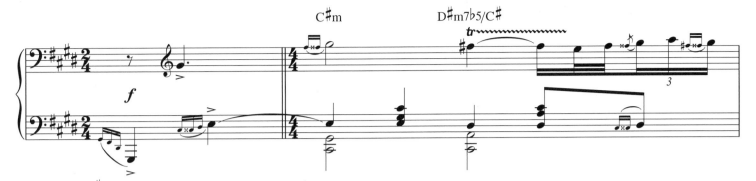

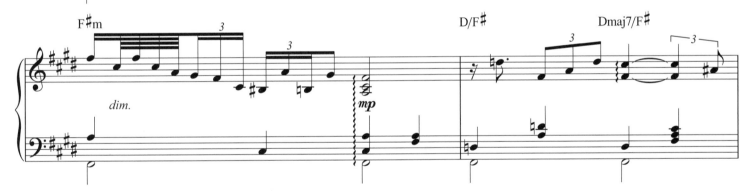

ST. JAMES INFIRMARY BLUES

By JOE PRIMROSE

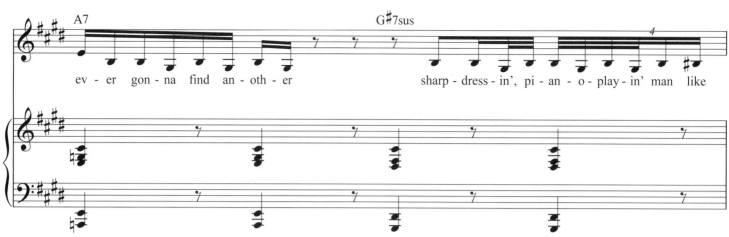

ev - er gon - na find an - oth - er sharp - dress - in', pi - an - o - play - in' man like

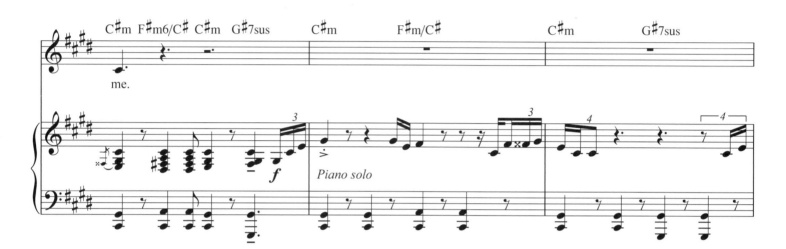

me.

Piano solo

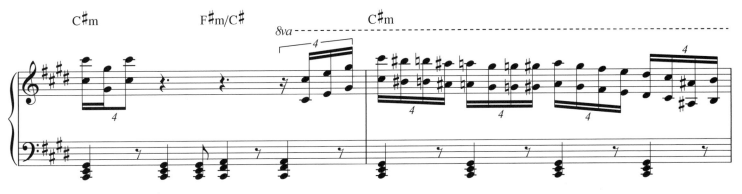

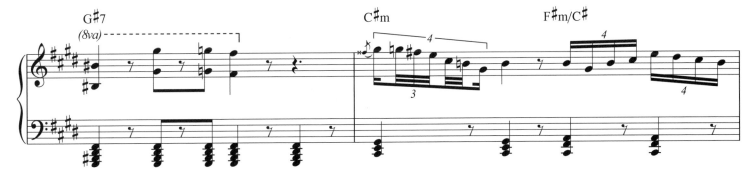

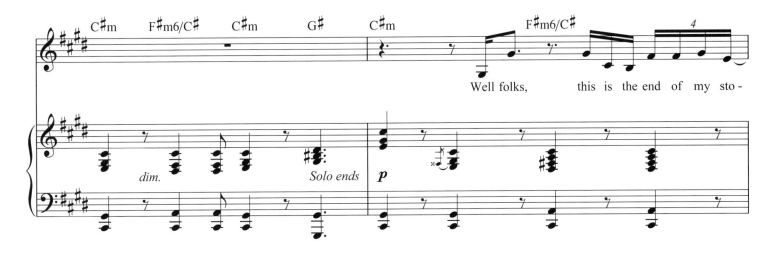

Well folks, this is the end of my sto-

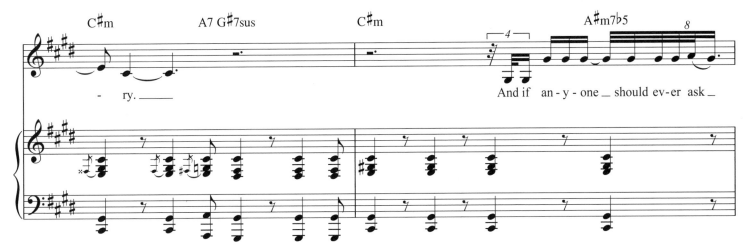

- ry. _____

And if an-y-one _ should ev-er ask _

you, ___ mm, ___ just go on a-head and tell ___

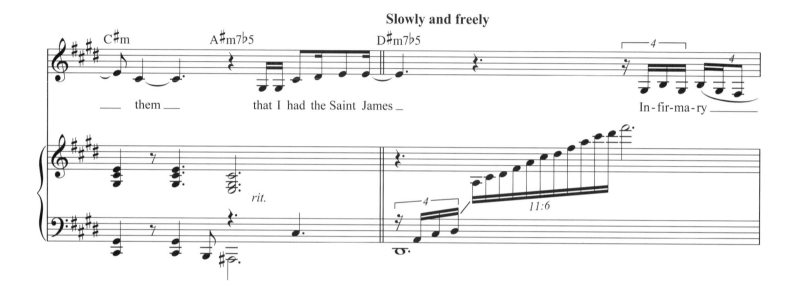

Slowly and freely

___ them ___ that I had the Saint James ___ In-fir-ma-ry ___

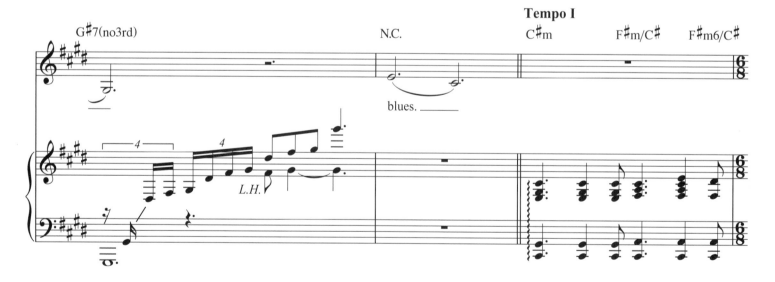

Tempo I

blues. ___

Freely

THE VERY THOUGHT OF YOU

Words and Music by
RAY NOBLE

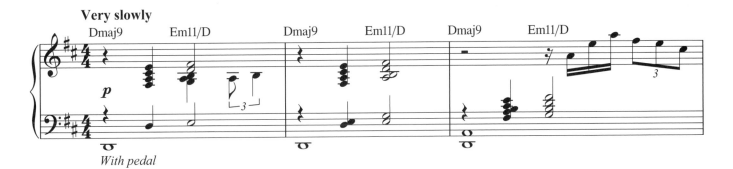

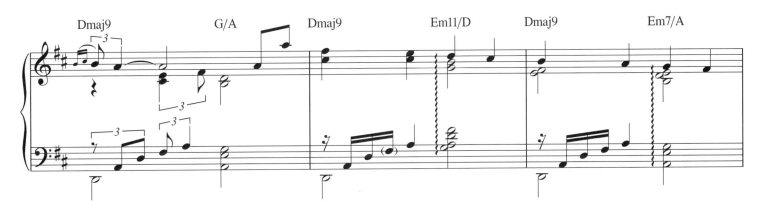

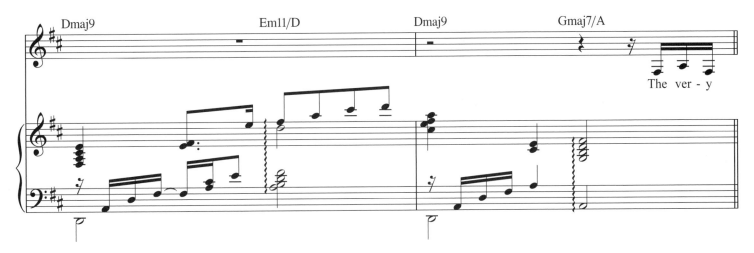

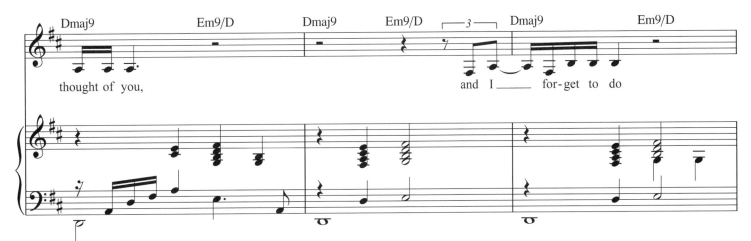

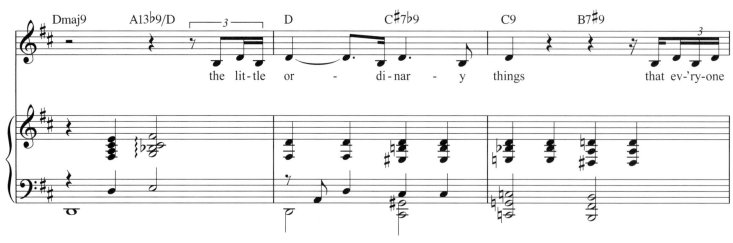

the lit-tle or - di-nar - y things that ev-'ry-one

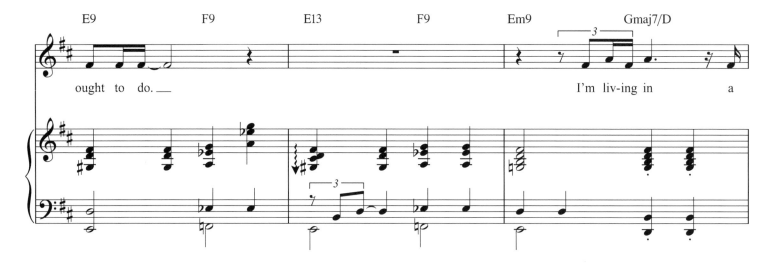

ought to do. ___ I'm liv-ing in a

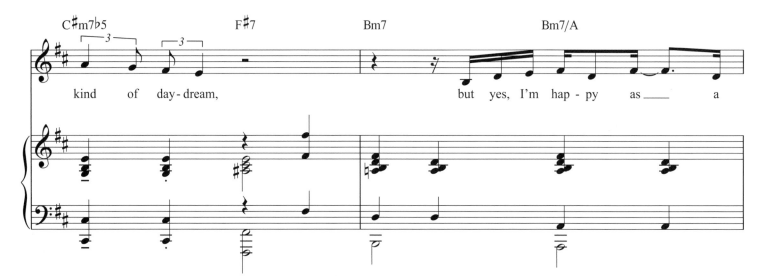

kind of day-dream, but yes, I'm hap-py as ___ a

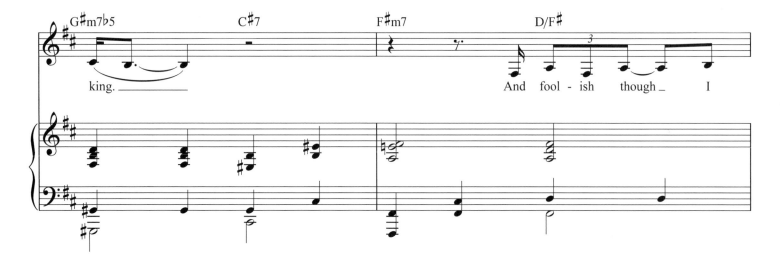

king. ___ And fool - ish though ___ I

may seem,   to me she's __ ev -'ry - thing.

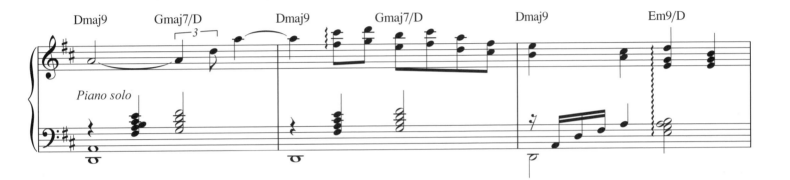

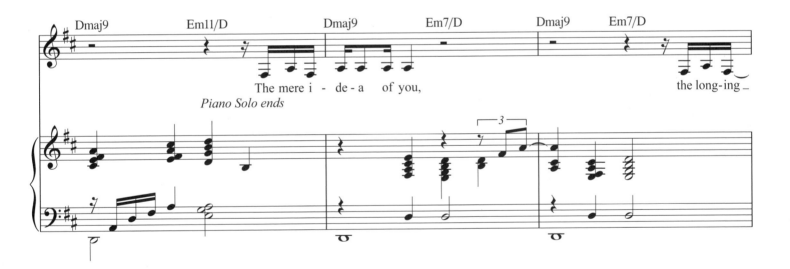

The mere i - de - a   of you,   the long-ing __

Piano Solo ends

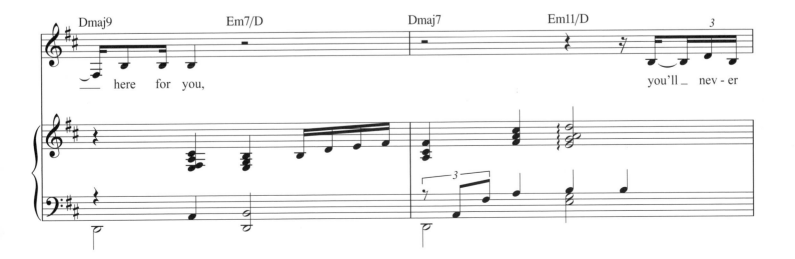

__ here for you,   you'll __ nev - er

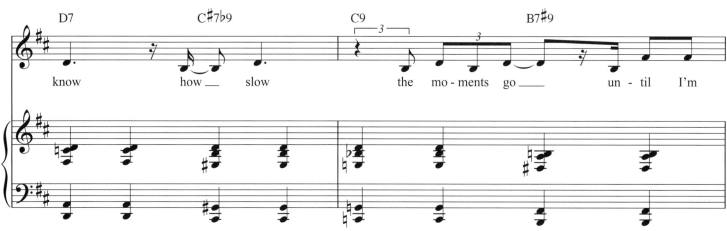

know how __ slow the mo - ments go __ un - til I'm

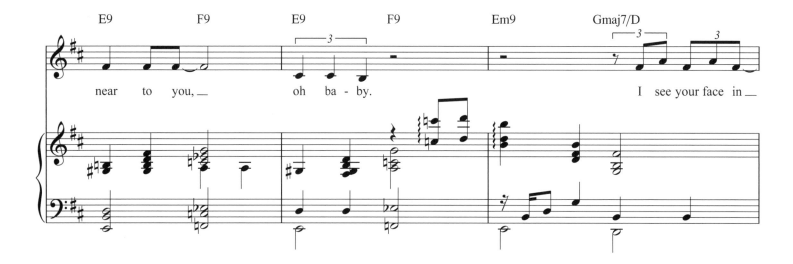

near to you, __ oh ba - by. I see your face in __

__ ev-'ry flow - er, and your eyes __ in stars __ a - bove. __

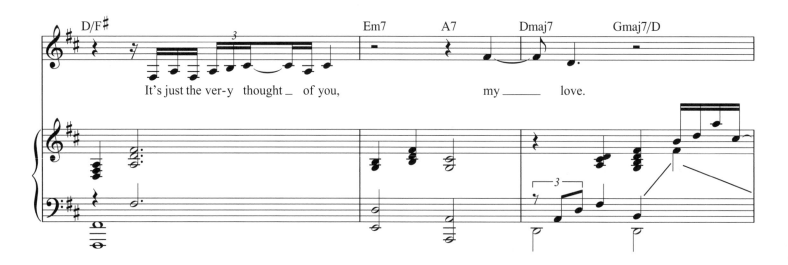

It's just the ver-y thought __ of you, my __ love.

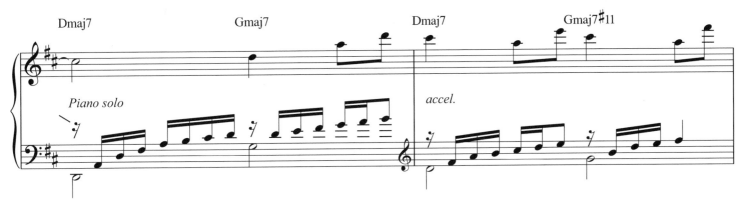

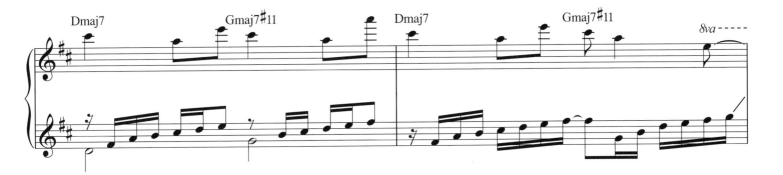

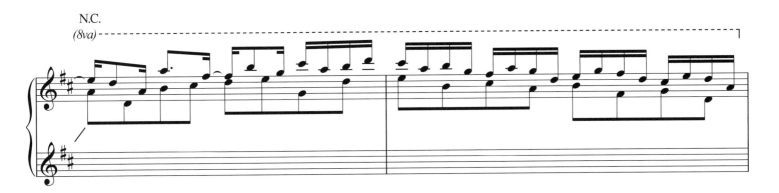

NOCTURNE NO. 1 IN D MINOR

Written by
JON BATISTE

Tango feel

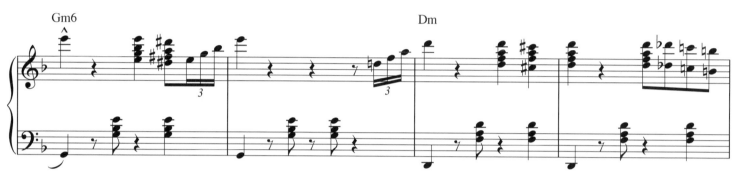

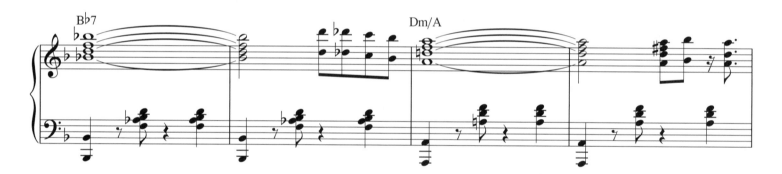

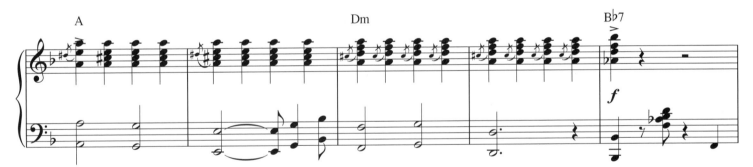

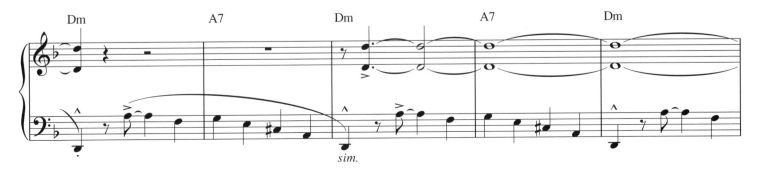

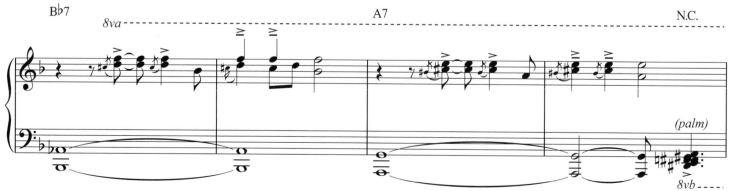

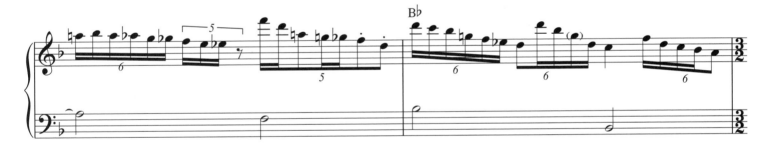

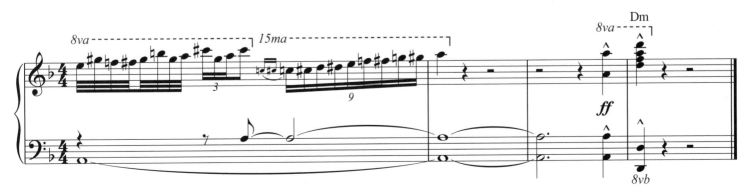

MR. BUDDY

Written by
JON BATISTE

Moderately, with freedom

Mis - ter Bud - dy was some-one who nev - er steered me wrong; he was al - ways sing - ing ___ a good song.

E - ven when some folks would hiss and jeer, he would-n't bend; ___

he was al - ways gon - na be him.

Whistle:

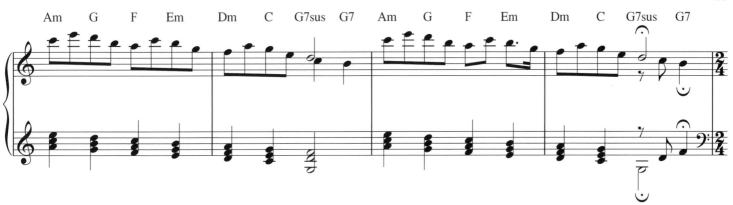

As the years went by, he did-n't need a pass of kin;

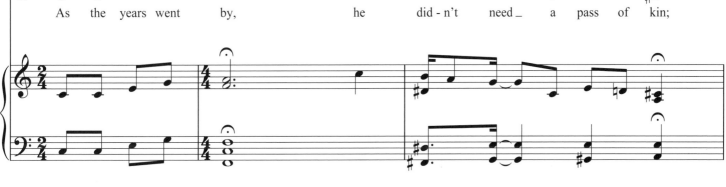

he was in the fam-'ly by then.

Piano Solo

Easy Swing

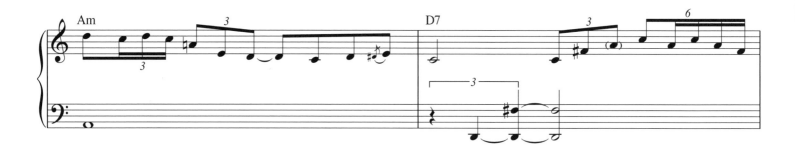

On the rail-road

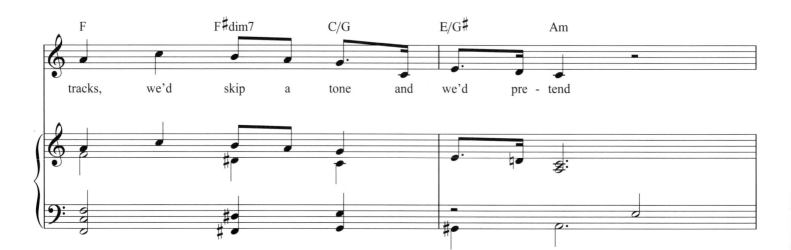

tracks, we'd skip a tone and we'd pre-tend

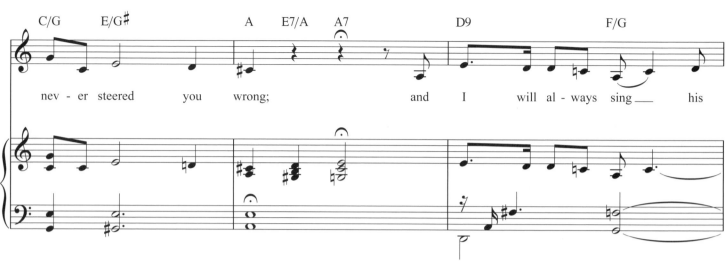

never steered you wrong; and I will always sing _____ his

song. _

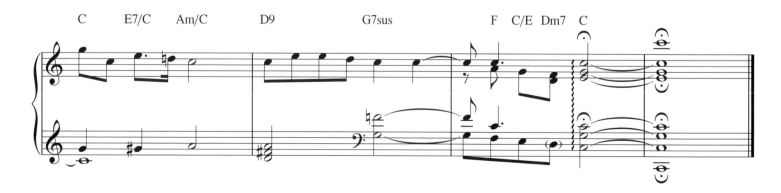

SMILE
Theme from MODERN TIMES

Words by JOHN TURNER
and GEOFFREY PARSONS
Music by CHARLES CHAPLIN

Slowly and freely

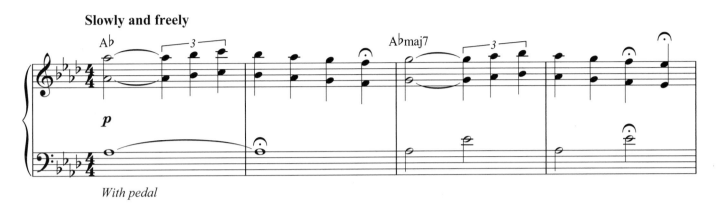

With pedal

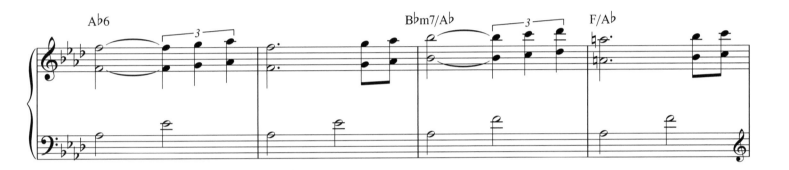

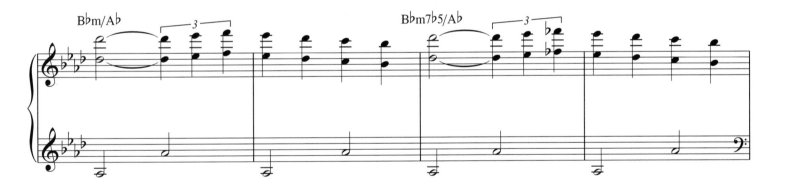

IS IT OVER

Written by
JON BATISTE

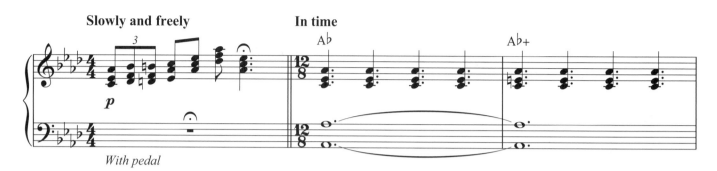

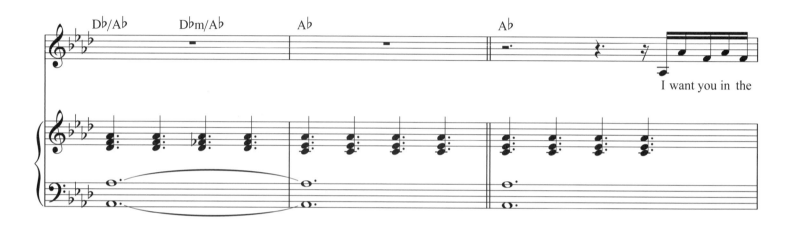

I want you in the

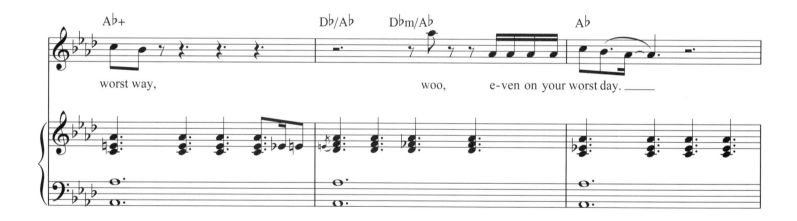

worst way,   woo,   e-ven on your worst day. ___

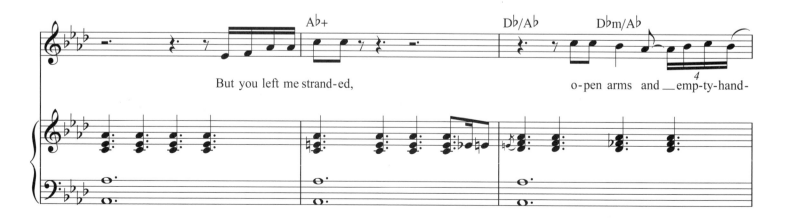

But you left me strand-ed,   o-pen arms and ___ emp-ty-hand-

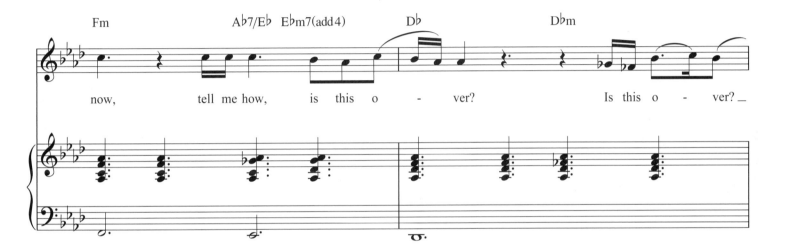

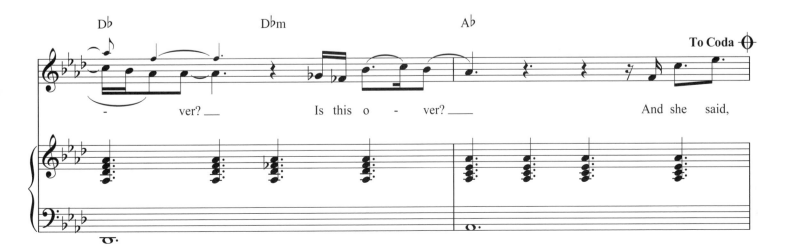

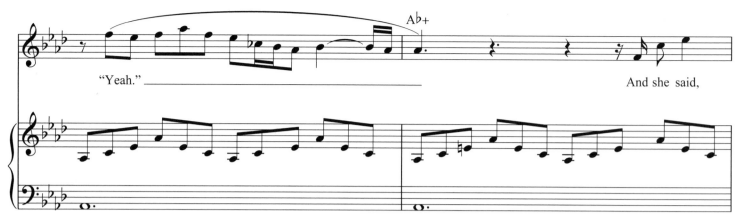

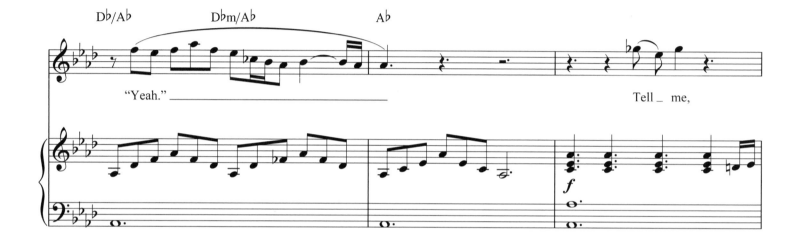

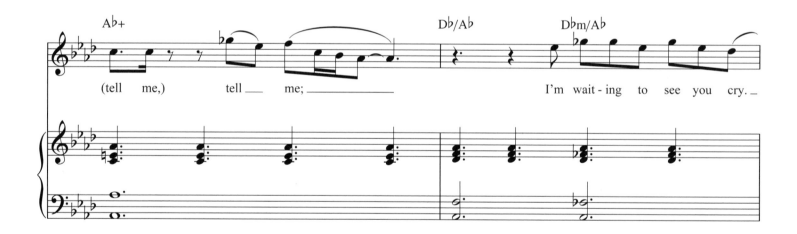

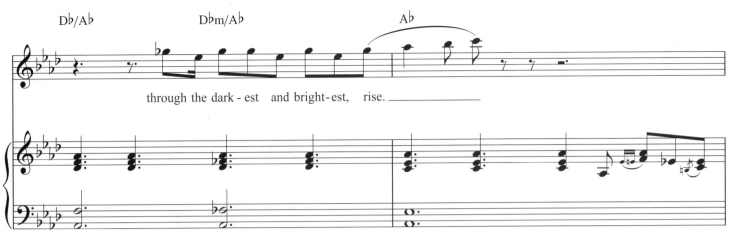

through the dark-est and bright-est, rise. _____

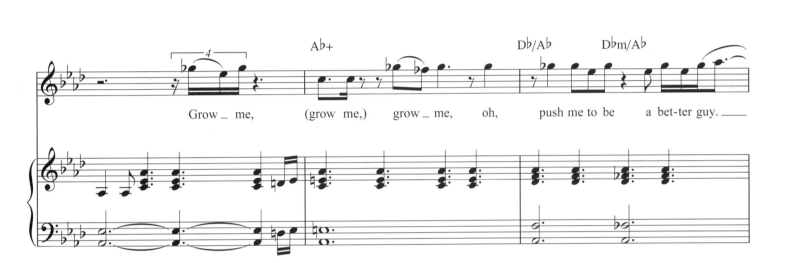

Grow _ me, (grow me,) grow _ me, oh, push me to be a bet-ter guy. _____

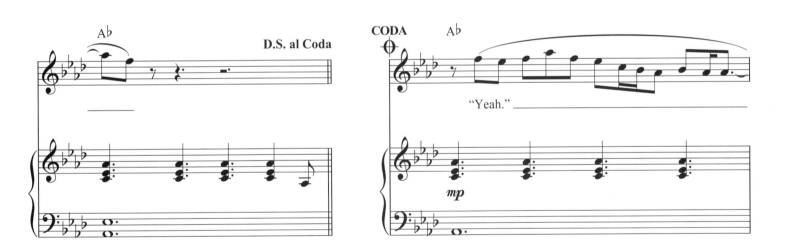

D.S. al Coda

CODA

"Yeah." _____

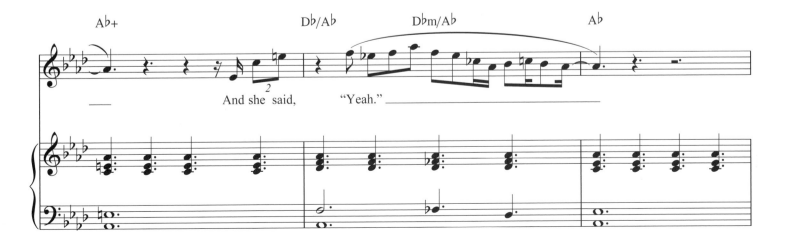

And she said, "Yeah." _____

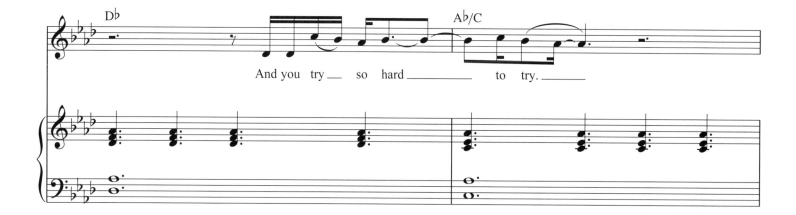

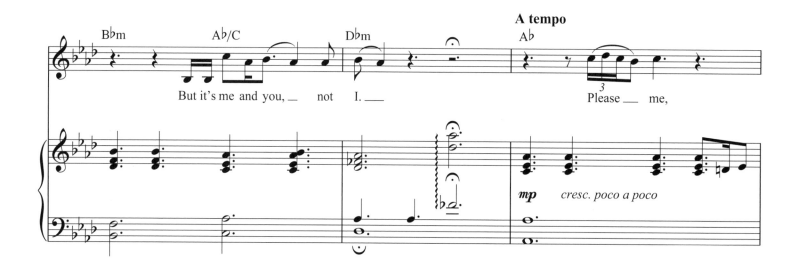

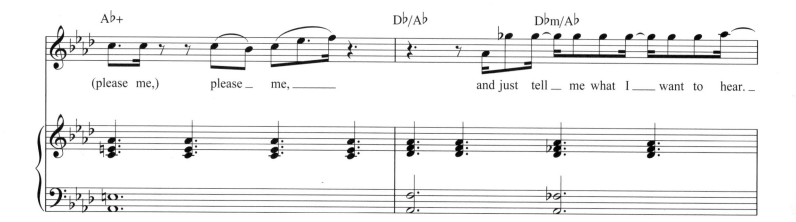

And she said, "Yeah."

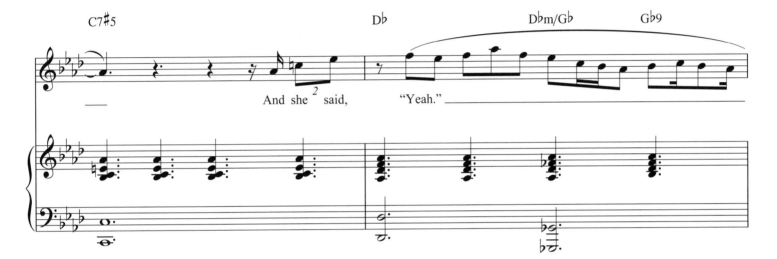

And she said, "Yeah."

And she said, "Yeah."

And she said, "Yeah."

DON'T STOP

Written by JON BATISTE
and STEVE McEWAN

Let's soak up the day, _____

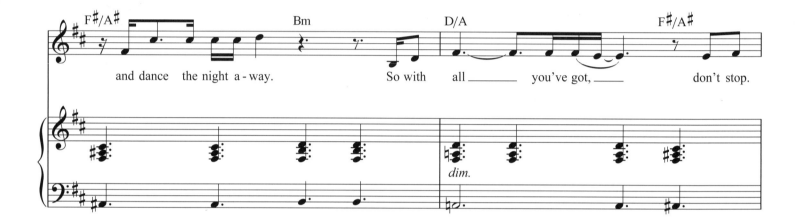

and dance the night a-way. So with all _____ you've got, _____ don't stop.

So with all you've got, _____ don't

stop.